HEINEMANN
STATE STUDIES

Virginia
Native Peoples

Karla Smith

Heinemann Library
Chicago, Illinois

© 2003 Heinemann Library
a division of Reed Elsevier Inc.
Chicago, Illinois

Customer Service 888-454-2279

Visit our website at www.heinemannlibrary.com

Designed by Heinemann Library
Page layout by Wilkinson Design
Printed and bound in the United States by
  Lake Book Manufacturing, Inc.

07 06 05 04 03
10 9 8 7 6 5 4 3 2 1

**Library of Congress
Cataloging-in-Publication Data**

Smith, Karla, 1947-
    Virginia's native peoples / Karla Smith.
      p. cm. -- (Heinemann state studies)
    Summary: Discusses the traditions, clothing, food,
    tools, and current status of the different tribes of
    Native Americans who made their home in what
    became the state of Virginia. Includes
    bibliographical references and index.
      ISBN 1-4034-0363-5 -- ISBN 1-4034-0585-9
    (pbk.)
      1. Indians of North America--Virginia--Juvenile
    literature.
    [1. Indians of North America--Virginia.]   I. Title.
    II. Series.
    E78.V7.S66 2003
    975.504'97--dc21

                              2002153001

Acknowledgments

The author and publishers are grateful to the
following for permission to reproduce copyright
material:

Cover photograph by (main) Alex Brandon/
Heinemann Library, (L-R) Ashmolean Museum/
University of Oxford, Alex Brandon/Heinemann
Library, Carl & Ann Purcell/Corbis, Alex Brandon/
Heinemann Library

Title page (L-R) Ashmolean Museum/University of
Oxford, The Mariner's Museum/Corbis, Michelle
Mouldenhauer/Archaeological Society of Virginia;
contents page (L-R) Virginia Historical Society,
Tony Belcastro, North Wind Picture Archives; p. 6
Carter Sisney; p. 7 Smithsonian Institution;
pp. 11T, 18, 19, 30 The Mariner's Museum/Corbis;
p. 11B Michelle Mouldenhauer/Archaeological
Society of Virginia; p. 12 Carnegie Museum of
Natural History; pp. 13, 14, 15, 16B, 17, 33 North
Wind Picture Archives; p. 16T Ashmolean
Museum/University of Oxford; p. 20 Color
lithograph by George Catlin, 1844 (based on a
sketch by George Catlin in the Fort Gibson area,
1834)/Illinois State Museum/Springfield, IL; pp. 25,
43 Alex Brandon/Heinemann Library; p. 27
Courtesy Frank H. McClung Museum/The
University of Tennessee; p. 31 Corbis; p. 32, 35
Bettmann/Corbis; p. 36 Reproduced by permission
of The Huntington Library, San Marino, California/
Accession Number: 9172; p. 37 Virginia Historical
Society; p. 38 Tony Belcastro; p. 39 Courtesy
Pepper Bird Foundation, S. Thomas; p. 41 Marilyn
"Angel" Wynn/Nativestock.com; p. 42 Denver
Art Museum

Photo research by Bobbie Schultz

Special thanks to Jean Hodges for her expert
advice on the series.

Every effort has been made to contact copyright
holders of any material reproduced in this book.
Any omissions will be rectified in subsequent
printings if notice is given to the publisher.

Some words are shown in bold, **like this.**
You can find out what they mean by looking
in the glossary.

Contents

The First People

The first people to live in present-day Virginia probably arrived here about 15,000 years ago. At that time, the earth's climate was colder than it is now. Much of North America was covered with thick, slow moving sheets of ice called glaciers. That time is known as the last **Ice Age.**

During the Ice Age, the level of the oceans dropped about 300 feet, because much of the water existed as ice in glaciers. Because the water level was lower, much of the seafloor was exposed as land. Between Asia and North America, the water level dropped enough to leave a land bridge.

Scientists think that the first people to **migrate** across the land bridge from Asia to North America were hunting. Groups of hunters and gatherers followed herds of animals they relied on for food, such as the woolly

American Indians believe their people have always been in the Americas. Evidence suggests that Paleo-Indians probably came from Asia, across the Bering Sea land bridge.

Migration Routes

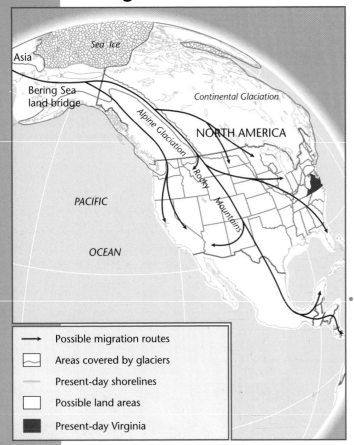

Asia
Sea Ice
Bering Sea land bridge
Continental Glaciation
Alpine Glaciation
NORTH AMERICA
Rocky Mountains
PACIFIC
OCEAN

→ Possible migration routes
Areas covered by glaciers
Present-day shorelines
Possible land areas
Present-day Virginia

mammoth. As they traveled south, they also gathered roots and berries for food. People probably migrated slowly over thousands of years. As the climate changed and began to warm up, the land bridge was covered by ocean water.

PALEO-INDIANS

Any period of time before written records of a group are kept is called prehistoric, meaning before history. Virginia's earliest peoples lived in three different time periods. The first one, the Paleo-Indian period, began 15,000 years ago when migrating hunters began arriving in Virginia. **Archaeologists** found **artifacts** of some of these hunters in a cave in southwest Virginia. These people lived in small groups and moved often to hunt and gather. Some groups may have returned to the same spot at the same time year after year, if the animals they hunted were there.

ARCHAIC PERIOD

The Archaic period began when the climate became warmer around 7000 B.C.E. By that time, plants had changed and many large animals had become **extinct.** New plants with fruit and nuts now grew. The American Indians of this period hunted deer, elk, bear, and moose. They made stone tools from **jasper** and river rock, and carved bowls from **soapstone.**

Cave Dwellers

Remains found in Virginia caves help us to know what Paleo-Indians ate. Their food included birds, fish, reptiles, **mussels,** and snails. Nutshells, seeds, and even corn were also found. The Paleo-Indians made stone tools and made clothes from animal hides. Some American Indians still lived in caves as late as the 1600s, when English settlers arrived.

Prehistoric Time Periods

PALEO-INDIANS	ARCHAIC	WOODLAND
13,000 B.C.E. to 7000 B.C.E.	7000 B.C.E. to 1000 B.C.E.	1000 B.C.E. to C.E. 1600

Spear and Atlatl

Spears were used mainly for hunting. The atlatl was a device that  helped a person throw a spear farther and faster. Atlatls were made of wood and had a hooked end. The hunter placed one end of the spear in the hooked end of the atlatl. With a flick of the arm, the hunter launched the spear. People as far back as the Archaic period used atlatls for hunting.

WOODLAND PERIOD

Indians of the Woodland period became farmers and began to live in permanent villages. With a more settled life, village groups became larger. People were able to develop better tools and technology since they no longer had to move constantly to follow the food supply.

Hundreds of low stone mounds have been found in the northern Shenandoah Valley. These mounds were burial places for Indians of the Woodland period. Because of the mounds, these Indians are often known as Stone Mound people. **Archaeologists** have found smoking pipes, copper beads, stone tools, weapons, and arrowheads in these mounds. Only important people in the tribe were buried in the mounds.

In the early part of the Woodland period, people lived in small villages along rivers. They hunted, fished, gathered plants, and farmed. They grew native plants like sunflowers, **gourds,** and squash. They preserved fish and deer meat by **smoking** it, so that they would have it during times when food was hard to find. They collected oysters from the coastal rivers. Woodland Indians made better tools than those of the Archaic period and began making pottery to use for cooking and storage. When Woodland Indians began to grow more food crops, their villages became larger and moved less often. The growing of more food allowed people to live in one place. Since there was more food, not everyone had to hunt or **forage** for food all the time. So, some people were free to become warriors or priests. Women had time to decorate their pottery and make jewelry. Coastal tribes made shell and pearl necklaces. The different Woodland Indian tribes traded with one another.

For hundreds of years, trade routes crisscrossed the Americas. Woodland Indians traded chunks of iron, crystals, **flints, turquoise,** shells, and **mica.** In Virginia, the most traveled route was the Great Warrior's Path. It was a main north-south route that connected the Iroquois tribes of the Great Lakes with those in the southeast, including the Cherokee. Traders from the different tribes of Virginia also traveled well-known paths between different regions. They traded goods and shared beliefs with the **cultures** of the Mississippi River and the Great Lakes Indians.

This shell pendant was found near the Potomac River. It was probably worn by an Indian of the Woodland period during ***ceremonies.***

THREE LANGUAGE GROUPS

The Coastal Plains, Piedmont, and Mountain-Valley areas developed cultures that matched their **environments.** These people were the groups that met the first European settlers in the 1600s.

By 1600, three Indian language groups had developed: Algonquian, Siouan, and Iroquoian. The tribes who spoke these languages lived in different regions of

Virginia. They claimed different areas for hunting and farming, and sometimes fought with one another over hunting ground rights.

Between 10,000 and 20,000 Algonquian speaking people lived in the Coastal Plains. Powhatan, a powerful chief, controlled 30 tribes. The Siouan speakers made up the next largest group. About 6,000 Siouan Indians from five tribes lived in the Piedmont region. The smallest group of American Indians was the Iroquoian speakers. There were about 2,500 Iroquois spread out in the far southwest Blue Ridge Mountains and along the Nottoway and Meherrin Rivers.

Pronunciations

Algonquian	=	Al GAHNG kee uhn
Siouan	=	SOO an
Iroquoian	=	Ihr uh KWOY an

Around 1600, American Indians of three language groups lived in Virginia. The Algonquian speakers (Powhatan) had the most contact with Europeans when they arrived, since they lived nearest the East Coast.

Three Language Groups

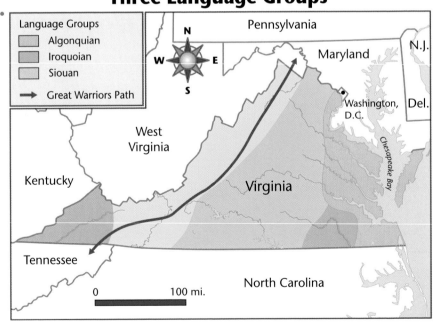

Language Groups
- Algonquian
- Iroquoian
- Siouan
→ Great Warriors Path

Pennsylvania
Maryland
N.J.
Washington, D.C.
Del.
West Virginia
Kentucky
Virginia
Chesapeake Bay
Tennessee
North Carolina

0   100 mi.

Powhatan: Algonquian Language Group

The Algonquian speakers of Virginia were known as the Powhatan (Pow uh TAN). A powerful chief in Virginia named Wahunsunacock **inherited** six tribes. He was known as a paramount chief, because he ruled

Algonquian/Powhatan Tribes

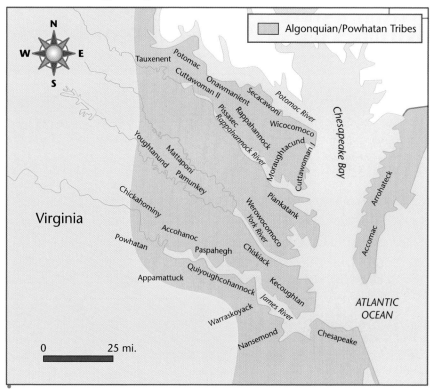

Chief Wahunsunacock (Powhatan) ruled over about 30 tribes in a kind of empire in Virginia's Coastal Plain. Villages were located on rivers because rivers were an important source of freshwater, food, and transportation.

Describing Powhatan

The English described the Powhatan as being "tall and straight." The average Powhatan was about six feet tall, which was taller than the average European in the 1600s. John Smith, an English colonist, wrote the following description of Chief Powhatan:

". . . He is of personage a tall well-proportioned man, with a sower looke, his head somewhat gray, his beard so thinne that it seemeth noe at al, his age neare 60; of a very able and hardy body to endure any labour."

over the chiefs of the individual tribes. The tribes Wahunsunacock ruled lived along the rivers of the Coastal Plain. His warriors conquered most other tribes along the Chesapeake Bay by 1600. Wahunsunacock's rule reached north to the Potomac River, west to the **fall line,** and south to the Dismal Swamp.

One of the tribes Wahunsunacock ruled was the Powhatan. *Powhatan* was also the name for the form of Algonquian language spoken by the tribes under Wahunsunacock's rule. After 1607, the English called Chief Wahunsunacock himself Powhatan, which became his most common name. So, both the chief and his empire of tribes became known as *Powhatan.*

A Powerful Ruler

Powhatan's position as chief was **inherited** through his mother, rather than father. Therefore, even though he had many children, they could not succeed him as chief. Instead, Powhatan's brothers, and then sisters, in order of age, would become chief after him.

Powhatan governed about 30 tribes, controlling more than 150 villages. He ruled by force and fear. Tribes that refused to be ruled by Powhatan were destroyed. Each of the tribes had its own district chief who reported directly to Powhatan. These tribes paid taxes to Powhatan in the form of baskets of corn, shell beads, deerskins, or whatever was valuable for trade. In return for the taxes, Powhatan and his warriors would protect the tribes.

SHELTER

Powhatan villages were usually surrounded by wooden fences that protected them from wild animals and enemy tribes. Some villages had as many as 100 homes. Villages were located on creeks and rivers. The Powhatan depended on canoes for transportation, but there were also footpaths on land used for fast communication between neighboring tribes. If the farm fields wore out, a village was moved.

Powhatan villages were protected by high wooden fences. The Powhatan also cut the grass outside the fences so that enemies could not sneak up on the village.

The main house of the Powhatan was the longhouse. More than one family shared a longhouse, which could be from 20 to 100 feet long. Powhatan women built the longhouses. They bent saplings, which are young trees, to form an arch, and tied them together with string made from animal muscle or plant **fiber.** Once the framework was finished, they covered the roof and sides with woven mats made of river **reeds** gathered in the **marsh.** When a village moved, the longhouses were left and Powhatan women built new ones at the next village location.

Small, round houses called *wigwams* were built for summer camps and hunting trips. They were made from the same materials as longhouses. In both types of house, a fire was kept burning at all times to keep away evil spirits.

Powhatan longhouses (top) and wigwams *(bottom) were very practical. They offered protection from outside weather, but could be easily rebuilt if the village had to move, since the materials could be easily found in the Coastal Plain. A lack of stone in the region also made wood the obvious choice for building.*

HUNTERS, GATHERERS, AND FARMERS

The Powhatan were hunters, gatherers, and farmers. The men hunted, and the women gathered food, grew crops, and cooked meals. In spring, the Powhatan collected wild greens and **tuckahoe.** In late summer, women and children collected food from the forest. They picked onions, plums, mulberries, strawberries, roots, pumpkins, and squash. In late fall, the entire tribe collected hickory nuts, walnuts, chestnuts, and acorns. Acorns were saved and used to make flour.

The Three Sisters

Corn, beans, and squash were planted in early summer. Seeds from all three were planted in small hills. The bean vines climbed the corn stalks, and the squash grew below. By midsummer, the fields looked overgrown with weeds but were actually filled with vegetables. The three crops growing together were called the three sisters.

Women also kept large gardens by their homes where they planted corn, beans, squash, peas, pumpkin, and sunflowers. Tobacco, which was used for ceremonies, was grown apart from the rest of the crops. The last of the crops were harvested in late fall and stored for winter. Powhatan women used pottery and baskets they made to hold and prepare the food they gathered and farmed.

Also during the late fall, entire villages went hunting. Men and boys hunted deer using bows and arrows. In addition, men made animal traps and used fire to drive animals out of the forest. Women and girls helped prepare the deer meat the men brought back. They scraped the skins and cut the meat into strips to be dried. The campsite was moved as the hunters found better hunting grounds.

The deer was the most important animal the Powhatan hunted. They used every part of the deer. Deerskins were made into clothing, and bones into tools. The deer meat was roasted and boiled, and some was dried and made into **jerky.** The Powhatan also hunted other forest animals, such as wild turkey, rabbit, and beaver. Every spring and fall, Indians hunted the wild ducks and geese that **migrated** through Virginia.

Fish were another important source of food for the Powhatan. They trapped migrating shad and sturgeon using nets made of strips of green oak and **reeds** woven

Powhatan hunters dressed in deerskins could walk right up to the deer. The Englishman John White observed this practice when he visited the coastal tribes in the 1580s.

When fishing at night from canoes, it was often the job of Powhatan boys and girls to keep the fire going in the center of the canoe.

together. The Powhatan also used nets to catch shellfish such as **mussels,** clams, and oysters, as well as crabs and turtles.

The Powhatan sometimes fished at night from their canoes. They would build a fire on top of stones in the middle of the canoe. Attracted to the fire, the fish would come to the top of the water. Then, one of the Powhatan fishers would spear the fish and bring it into the canoe. The Powhatan also used hooks they made from fish bones to catch fish.

CLOTHING AND ACCESSORIES

The Powhatan did not wear much clothing. Almost all clothing the Powhatan men, women, and children did wear was made from the skins of animals. Deerskin was used most often. Women prepared the deerskins the men brought back from the hunt. They scraped the skin and made it soft. Then they cut it into pieces to be sewn with needles made of bone. The stringy muscles of the deer, called sinew, were pulled apart and used for thread. All Powhatan usually wore moccasins made of **buckskin.** Both men and women wore leggings made of animal skin to protect their legs when they traveled in the forest.

Powhatan men usually wore a loincloth made of animal skin between the thighs. They wore some jewelry, including earings, usually made from shells or bones. The men pulled back their long hair on the left side into a knot decorated with shells and feathers. They shaved their hair on the right side of the head where they used their bows, so that the bowstring wouldn't get caught in their hair. Powhatan men used body paint when preparing for war or games. Important men wore a type of shirt made of deerskin or turkey feathers. Chiefs wore decorative clothes and ornaments made of pearl, rare shell beads, and copper, which was a valuable metal to the Powhatan.

Powhatan women wore skirts made of deerskin. Married women wore their hair long and braided in the back. Young girls shaved their hair close on the front and sides, with the rest of the hair growing long and braided in the back. Women tattooed a large portion of their bodies with designs of flowers, fruits, and snakes and other animals. They also wore jewelry, including necklaces and bracelets, usually made of shells. The quality of a woman's jewelry showed how important she or her husband was in the community.

Sunscreen

Virginia Indians may have used the first sunscreen. The orange-red sap of the bloodroot plant was mixed with bear grease and rubbed on the skin. This protected the skin from the sun and kept a person cool in summer and warm in winter. Indians also used the sap of the bloodroot as war paint.

The rich cloth and fringes of this woman's skirt and her necklaces show other Powhatan men and women that she is married to a chief.

Powhatan's Mantel

Chief Powhatan is supposed to have owned a cape of deerskin that was sewn with thousands of tiny shells. These shells represented the tribes he controlled. The cape, called a mantel, is now owned by the Ashmolean Museum in Oxford, England.

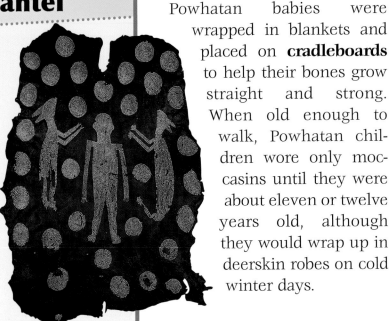

Powhatan babies were wrapped in blankets and placed on **cradleboards** to help their bones grow straight and strong. When old enough to walk, Powhatan children wore only moccasins until they were about eleven or twelve years old, although they would wrap up in deerskin robes on cold winter days.

RELIGION AND RITUAL

The Powhatan believed in many gods. They believed the gods controlled such things as floods, sickness, the growth of crops, animals, and water. A special house called a *quioccosan* was built in the village where offerings were made to the gods. Carved wooden posts would often be placed near the *quioccosan* for special dances. The Powhatan also worshiped the sun. Each morning they sprinkled tobacco on the river to honor the sun. Tobacco was used in many other types of **ceremonies** as well. The Powhatan believed in an

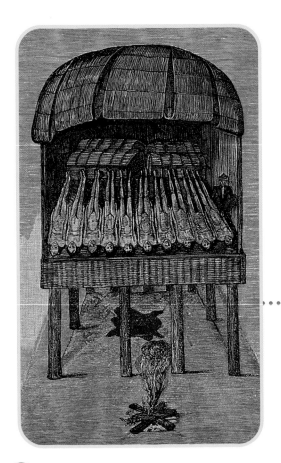

Each Powhatan village had a special house where the bodies of dead chiefs were preserved and laid out for all to see. Fires were always kept burning and the bodies were guarded, to make sure the chiefs would have a safe and happy afterlife.

A Powhatan medicine man was as important and respected as the chief. Only the medicine man knew the special herbs, roots, and words that could heal the sick. The special hairstyle and shirt showed the medicine man's importance.

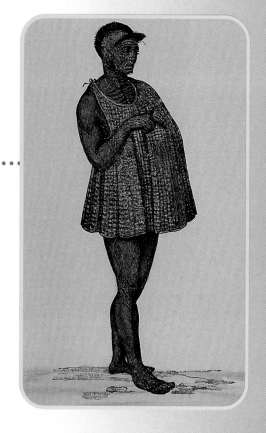

afterlife. They preserved the bodies of important people in a special house. Fires were kept going, and the house was guarded to insure a safe afterlife for the dead.

The medicine man of a tribe had special knowledge of plants and **herbs.** He was the "doctor" or healer of the tribe. Medicine and religion were related, and both required a strong belief in the gods. Most villages had a **sweat lodge,** and the medicine men believed sweating would cure most illnesses.

Between the ages of ten and fifteen, Powhatan boys went through a trial of manhood called a *huskanawing.* Boys had to be chosen for the *huskanawing* by the men of the tribe. The *huskanawing* included a village ceremony of song and dance. After this, the boys were expected to go out and survive alone in the forest for as many as nine months! They had to use the hunting skills they had learned to stay alive. Upon their return, the young men who survived the *huskanawing* would be honored by the village and their hair would be cut like the Powhatan men. They were now considered men by the tribe. They could marry, would be expected to bring back food from a hunt, and would go to war when necessary.

The Algonquian-speaking Powhatan did not make their girls go through a *huskanawing.* A twelve-year-old

Canoes

The dugout canoe was very important in Powhatan life. Canoes were used for travel, to carry things, and for fishing. They could be as small as eight to ten feet long, or large enough to carry as many as 40 people.

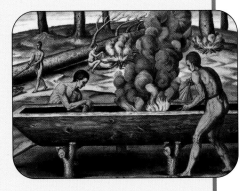

To make a canoe, the Powhatan would build a fire at the base of a wide tree trunk in order to make it fall. They would then burn out a long hole down the center of the tree trunk while also scraping the bark and wood away. The Powhatan rubbed bear grease on the smooth wood to keep it from rotting. They used wooden paddles or poles to make the canoe move.

Powhatan girl would be considered a woman once she could do the work of a woman well. At that point, she would be given the clothes of a woman, and could have tattoos like a woman.

Parents arranged the marriage of a daughter. A man would have to pay a price set by the family to marry their daughter. The price of the bride was usually paid in deerskins, beads, copper, or other items considered valuable. When the price had been paid, the girl's parents brought her to the groom's home for a wedding **ceremony** and feast. A girl might be married as early as age thirteen, and a young man as early as age fifteen.

MAKING USE OF THE ENVIRONMENT

Powhatan men were ready for war at any time. Powhatan warriors fought in large groups and conducted small raids and surprise attacks. The bow and arrow served as the main tool and weapon of Powhatan men. They often used the wood of a young green locust tree to make bows. Arrows were made from strong **reeds**. The Powhatan traded for stone arrowheads or made them from sharp animal bones or shells. War clubs, which

The bow and arrow was the main weapon and tool of Powhatan men. For arrow points, the Powhatan sometimes used a sharp bone from a turkey leg or a sharp bill from a bird. Turkey feathers helped arrows fly straight. Quivers were made from animal skins.

were strong sticks with a stone tied to one end, were used in hand-to-hand combat.

The Powhatan people played music and danced for religious ceremonies and entertainment. They collected things from their **environment,** such as **gourds** and river **canes,** to make drums, rattles, and other instruments to use in their dances and songs.

FUN AND GAMES

Tribes competed in sporting events, too. A game similar to **lacrosse** was played by men, and a game similar to soccer was played by the women and children. Men challenged each other to footraces, boxing, and wrestling. One of the most popular games played by the men was a guessing game using 81 straws. Players **gambled** as they tried to guess the number of straws other players held.

*Powhatan men played a game similar to **lacrosse**. Teams used stringed rackets to carry or throw a ball toward a goal. Racket strings were made with animal sinew. The ball was usually made of wood.*

Powhatan children often played some form of tag. Girls had **cornhusk dolls** and made bowls from clay. Boys played with bows and arrows. Even in their play, Powhatan boys and girls were learning the skills they would need to survive as adults in the tribe. All children played in the river and learned to swim and paddle canoes. Girls and boys needed canoeing skills for fishing and collecting food.

THE POWHATAN TODAY

The Powhatan Empire did not survive long once Europeans were determined to colonize Virginia. However, seven of the eight tribes that are recognized by Virginia today were originally part of the Powhatan Empire.

Siouan Language Group

Virginia American Indians who lived west of the **fall line** spoke the Siouan language. The fall line separates the Piedmont and Tidewater regions of Virginia, where the fresh water flowing east drops off to meet with the sea water coming in from the ocean. Virginia's Siouan tribes probably traded with each other, and occasionally with the Powhatan, although they also fought with the Powhatan. There were many fewer Siouan Indians than Powhatan, and they had much less power in the region.

SAPONI CONFEDERATION

The Saponi, Occaneechi, and Tutelo tribes all spoke the Siouan language and were similar in the way they lived. In 1713, a treaty brought them all together under the name Saponi **Confederation. Ancestors** of these tribes settled east of the Blue Ridge Mountains. They built their villages in the land they called *Ahkontshuck,* which means "high or hilly land." Today, we know this region as the Virginia Piedmont.

Within their villages, the Saponi lived in circular houses very similar to the Algonquian *wigwams.* These could be easily moved and rebuilt if the tribe moved. A wooden frame was shaped and then was covered with bark and animal skins. The floor of the house was also covered with animals skins, as well as **rush** mats.

Like the Powhatan, chiefs of the Saponi Confederation **inherited** their positions through the mother, rather

Pronunciations

Saponi	=	Sa PON ee
Occaneechi	=	O can EE chee
Tutelo	=	TU te lo
Manahoac	=	Man uh HO ack
Monacan	=	MON uh can

than the father. The roles of men and women were basically the same as with the Algonquian Powhatan. Men were warriors and hunters, and women did the gathering and farming. Saponi boys had to participate in a coming-of-age **ritual** similar to the Powhatan in order to become men of the tribe.

The Saponi grew a variety of crops, including corn, squash, **gourds,** and several kinds of beans and fruit. They also gathered nuts, wild parsnips, turnips, and other plants. Deer were an important source of meat and hides. Saponi men also hunted bears, beavers, opossums, raccoons, rabbits, turkeys, and a variety of fish.

*The Virginia **fall line** acted as a natural boundary, with the Siouan tribes living west of it and the Powhatan to the east. That way the two groups each had their own hunting grounds and could usually live in peace.*

Siouan Tribes

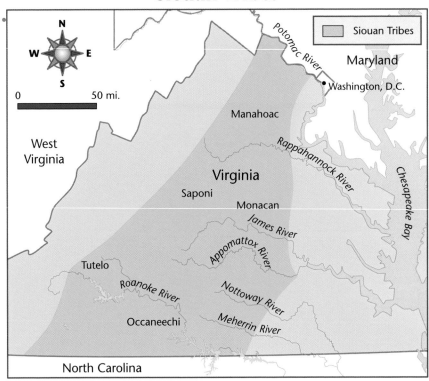

Tribes of the Iroquoian nation to the north raided Saponi tribes. English settlers arriving in the 1600s also took their lands. In the early 1700s, the Saponi finally made peace with the Iroquois north of Virginia and many moved to Iroquoian territory. Others decided to stay in Virginia. Governor Spotswood built a trading post at Fort Christianna in 1713, where he also started a **reservation** for the Siouan tribes and a school for their children.

Only a few members of the Saponi **Confederation** remained in southern Virginia through the years. They were part of the Occaneechi Tribe. Many of these families took English names and were able to gain back some of their land. Most of the Occaneechi moved south into North Carolina by the end of the 1700s. Today, they are organized as the Occaneechi Band of the Saponi Nation in Mebane, North Carolina. The tribe continues to work to preserve its history and **traditions.**

MANAHOAC

The English captain John Smith met Manahoacs while exploring the Rappahannock River in 1608. No Europeans ever visited a Manahoac village, so we know very little about the Manahoac people.

Like the Powhatan, the Manahoac people were hunters, gatherers, and farmers. They made similar clothing, shelter, and tools using the things they found in nature. European explorers could not find any Monahoac towns in 1669, even though John Smith had mentioned one in his notes. Most of the tribes had moved by then, possibly because of attacks from other tribes to the north. Diseases that were brought by the English, and for which the American Indians had no resistance, may have reduced the number of Manahoacs as well. A small population of Manahoacs remained in Virginia, but there was no major tribe or group by the end of the 1600s.

Natural Bridge

According to legend, the Monacan Indians discovered Natural Bridge while under attack by Algonquian tribes. When the Monacans reached the **chasm** of Cedar Creek, without a visible way to cross over, they knelt down and prayed for the Great Spirit to protect them. When they arose from praying, the bridge had appeared. Women and children crossed to safety. With renewed strength and courage, the men followed, but not until after they met and defeated the Algonquins.

MONACAN

The Monacans were friends with the Manahoac tribes. The Monacans had open settlements, though, unlike the Powhatan villages that were surrounded by walls made up of tree trunks. Like the Powhatan, the Monacans survived on Virginia's wildlife; however, there is evidence that they relied more heavily on farming and less on gathering than the Algonquian speakers. Like other Siouan and Algonquian tribes, the Monacan grew tobacco for use in **ceremonies.**

Because of the increasing number of European settlers coming into their territory, the Monacans began leaving their hunting and fishing grounds near the end of the 1600s. In 1669, the Monacan population in Virginia had decreased to a total of 120 people. By 1700, European colonists in the area found that the five known Monacan towns were empty. In the 1980s, the Monacan Indians reclaimed their homeland at Bear Mountain. Today, the Monacan Tribe is one of the eight recognized tribes of Virginia.

Iroquoian Language Group

There were three main tribes of the Iroquoian language group that lived in Virginia. A group of Cherokee lived in the southwest corner of Virginia. The Meherrin lived in the southeastern part of Virginia. And the third tribe, the Nottoway, lived near the Meherrin in southeastern Virginia.

CHEROKEE

A group of Cherokee Indians lived in the southwestern mountains of Virginia at one time. However, by the time European explorers and settlers made their way to the

Iroquoian Tribes

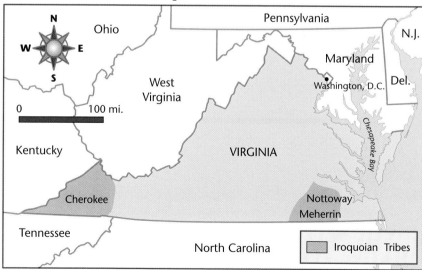

There was probably a total of about 2,500 people living among the three Iroquoian tribes of Virginia in the 1500s.

southwest corner of Virginia in the 1700s, the Indian villages were empty. A **surveyor** for the Royal Land Company came across an abandoned village in 1750. He described what he saw: ". . . In the Fork between Holston and the North River, are five Indian Houses built with logs and covered with bark, and there were an abundance of Bones, some whole Pots and Pans, some broken and many pieces of mats and Cloth."

Cherokee tribes lived in towns along rivers. People lived in family **clans** and helped make council decisions. Cherokee clans were usually named after animals, including the wolf, deer, bird, and turtle. Men and women of the same clan were not allowed to marry each other. As with the Algonquian and Siouan tribes, Cherokee men were warriors and hunters, and the women gathered food and grew crops. They gathered and grew basically the same foods as the Powhatan, with the exception of the fish found only near the ocean.

The Cherokee ruled themselves a bit differently than the Algonquian and Siouan speakers. Rather than having one chief rule, a group of **elders** made decisions for the tribe. The whole village could attend the meeting of the council of elders, which took place in a large council house located in the center of each village. The council house was the center of all tribal **ceremonies.** There were two elected chiefs in each town, a peace chief and a war chief, who had more power than others in the village. The peace chief was usually one of the elders of the tribe, and the war chief was a younger, successful warrior. Although they could not be chiefs, women could rise to positions of importance and have a great influence on the tribe's decisions.

Pronunciations

Cherokee	=	CHAIR uh kee
Nottoway	=	NOT uh way
Meherrin	=	Muh HAIR in

This drawing shows what the Cherokee winter home (left) and summer home (right) looked like and how they were made.

Because of the cold mountain climate, the Cherokee in Virginia built two types of houses for different seasons. Their summer homes were built with poles, woven twigs, and a type of clay plaster. During the winter season, they lived in round earthen lodges, each warmed by a small fire.

NOTTOWAY AND MEHERRIN

The Nottoway and Meherrin people also spoke the Iroquoian language and had very similar lifestyles and customs to each other and to other Virginia tribes of all languages. They lived in the Coastal Plain and Piedmont regions of Virginia along the Nottoway and Meherrin Rivers. In the 1600s, travel on water was the best way to go somewhere. Since the Nottoway and Meherrin Rivers did not connect to the Chesapeake Bay directly, early English settlers at Jamestown had very little contact with them. The Dismal Swamp helped somewhat to keep the Algonquian Powhatan from bothering the Nottoway and Meherrin as well.

Unlike the Algonquian speaking Powhatan, whose towns were organized under one powerful chief, the Nottoway and Meherrin lived as tribes in independent villages. Each of these villages had its own local chief who had little power beyond the village.

Villages themselves were made up of longhouses and gardens, and were surrounded by a tall protective wall, very much like the Powhatan. The Nottoway and Meherrin houses were made in the same way, and with the same materials, as the houses of the Algonquian speaking Powhatan. Nottoway and Meherrin men and women did the same work as the Algonquian and Siouan men and women. The men hunted the same kinds of animals, and the women farmed the same types of crops and gathered the same kinds of plants, nuts, and fruits as the Powhatan.

By 1650, participation in the fur trade had increased the Nottoway and Meherrin contact with the English settlers in Virginia. However, in a treaty with the settlers in 1677, the Nottoway and Meherrin lost their lands. Some moved further inland to new settlements along the Nottoway River. They continued to lose their lands as more European settlers arrived to start **plantations.** By the 1800s, the Nottoway and Meherrin tribes had basically disappeared. It is likely that many of the Iroquoian speakers left the area after hearing about diseases and conflicts caused by the European settlers as well. Today, only **artifacts** found along the streams and rivers are evidence that they were there.

European Settlers Change Virginia

European explorers and settlers wanted to get rich quick by finding gold and silver in Virginia. When they did not find gold and silver, rich farmland became the most valuable resource for the English settlers in Jamestown in the 1600s. Tobacco became an important crop. However, the first settlers experienced many hardships and had to rely on the Algonquian speaking Powhatan in order to survive.

Virginia American Indians believed that no one person "owned" land. They believed that all unoccupied land was for hunting and gathering. They cared about the health of the forest because it was their source of food, clothing, and shelter.

European settlers held very different beliefs. Private ownership of land was very important to them. Europeans used the forest as a supply of lumber and fur. They killed many animals to sell their fur, and they cut down trees to turn the land into tobacco fields. In this way, European settlers would change the land of Virginia.

JOHN WHITE IN VIRGINIA

In 1584, Queen Elizabeth I sent English explorers to find gold and places to build settlements in North America. Artist John White was part of that group. While he was in the Virginia region, White made many drawings and paintings of the coastal Algonquian Indians. White is not a perfectly accurate source, but his art at least gives us some idea of what those native peoples looked like.

*This drawing is of a Powhatan **elder** dressed for winter. Many drawings like this have been based on the original drawings of John White. Through his drawings we have a better idea of what the Powhatan he saw looked like.*

DISEASE

Throughout the 1600s, more and more European settlers came to Virginia. American Indian tribes in Virginia began dying from European diseases, such as **smallpox,** mumps, measles, and even chicken pox. Often, within a few days after the English had contact with a tribe, **epidemics** would break out.

The native people had no **immunity** to European diseases because they had not encountered them before. They did not understand what was happening to them. Whole villages died when stricken with these diseases. In just 100 years, the population of Virginia's American Indians was reduced from about 30,000 to about 1,000.

POWHATAN AND JOHN SMITH

Pocahontas was one of the favorite daughters of Chief Powhatan. In 1607, when she was about twelve years old, she met the English explorer, John Smith. Smith was on a trading trip on the Chickahominy River when he was captured by the Powhatan. After being led from village to village, he was brought to the village of Chief Powhatan.

Chief Powhatan asked Smith what the English were doing in his land. Smith told him that their ship had been damaged and that they were waiting for another ship to take them back to England. Smith explained that he was looking for the passage to the Pacific Ocean.

Powhatan did not hurt John Smith. Instead, he made him an adopted member of his tribe. Powhatan even wanted Smith to move to Capahowasick, a nearby Powhatan town. But John Smith returned to Jamestown. He was only there a few days when a fire broke out. Jamestown burned, and all of the food supplies were destroyed. John Smith then returned to Powhatan's village to trade for food.

The English captain John Smith claimed that Pocahontas, a daughter of Chief Powhatan, saved him from being killed by the Powhatan.

POWHATAN SAVES JAMESTOWN, 1608

All through the winter of 1608, the English needed food. Pocahontas became a messenger for her father. Chief Powhatan sent "bread, fish, turkies, squirrels, deare and other wilde beasts" to Jamestown. He wanted tools and guns in return for the food. It didn't take long before supplies became low in the Powhatan villages, too. At that point, the colonists often forced the tribes to give them food.

31

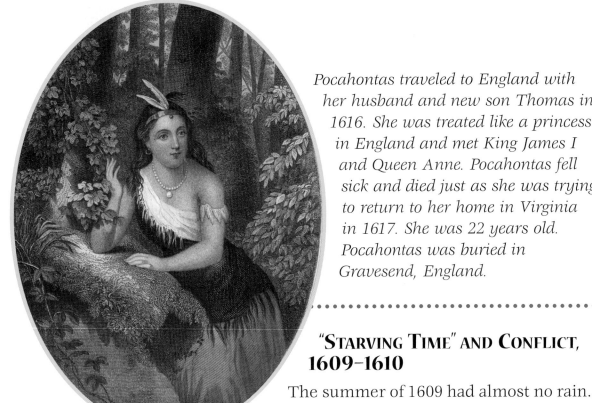

Pocahontas traveled to England with her husband and new son Thomas in 1616. She was treated like a princess in England and met King James I and Queen Anne. Pocahontas fell sick and died just as she was trying to return to her home in Virginia in 1617. She was 22 years old. Pocahontas was buried in Gravesend, England.

"STARVING TIME" AND CONFLICT, 1609–1610

The summer of 1609 had almost no rain. This led to an even greater shortage of food. The colonists kept demanding more food from the Powhatan, who barely had enough for themselves. This led to more fighting between the English colonists and the American Indians. When John Smith was injured in 1609 and had to return to England, Jamestown lost its best trader. The winter of 1609–1610 became known as the Starving Time for both the American Indians and the colonists. By March of 1610, the population of the Jamestown colony had decreased from 500 to 60.

Powhatan's tribes and the Jamestown colonists fought for several years. The colonists thought they had a right to take the Powhatan land. The Powhatan were beginning to understand that the English were here to stay.

POCAHONTAS PEACE, 1614

In 1613, an English sea captain kidnapped Pocahontas and took her to Jamestown. The English thought Chief Powhatan, her father, would return some guns to get her back, but Powhatan refused to do that. Pocahontas lived in Jamestown and learned the English ways. She married an English colonist named John Rolfe in 1614. Pocahontas's marriage to John Rolfe helped the English make peace with Chief Powhatan and his people.

OPECHANCANOUGH

Chief Powhatan's tribes lived in peace with the colonists after Pocahontas's wedding. In 1618, Chief Powhatan died. His brothers, first Opichapam and then Opechancanough, took over as chief of the Powhatan people. When Opechancanough became chief, he decided the English had been in the land of the Powhatan long enough. The peace between the Powhatan and the colonists would soon end.

Opechancanough spoke out against the Virginia colonists and gained the support of his warriors. But even his attacks could not stop more Europeans from settling in Virginia.

In 1622, Opechancanough led an attack to drive the colonists from Virginia. It has been called the "Massacre of 1622." About 340 of the 1,200 settlers along the James River were killed. Despite this attack, new ships arrived each month with more European settlers eager for land to farm. By 1644, there were about 15,000 settlers along the Virginia coastal rivers. Opechancanough led a second attack that year, and about 1,200 colonists were killed. The colonists struck back and, by 1646, Opechancanough was captured and taken to Jamestown. He was killed while being held prisoner.

TREATIES MADE AND BROKEN

The colonists made several treaties with American Indians. However, more colonists continued to arrive

Colonial Census Figures

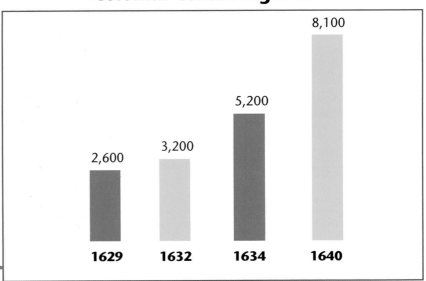

*Colonial **census** figures clearly show how quickly the number of European settlers in Virginia grew. As the number of European settlers grew, so did tension between them and the Powhatan.*

and start farms and **plantations** on American Indian land, breaking those treaties. The Powhatan struggled to survive after Opechancanough's death in 1646. The new chief, Necotowance, signed a treaty that put him under the control of the king of England. Tribes lost most of their lands to settlers. New laws said that the American Indians were not allowed to travel in colonial settlements without badges or permission. As more Europeans came, the frontier settlements spread west into the Piedmont region of Virginia.

BACON'S REBELLION, 1676

In 1676, colonial **militiamen** mistakenly attacked a friendly group of Iroquoian speaking Indians who had come south into the Virginia Piedmont. The Indians responded to this attack by raiding settlements along the Piedmont frontier. One of the **plantations** they attacked belonged to Nathaniel Bacon. Bacon asked the governor of Virginia to send help to fight the American Indians. When Governor Berkeley refused, Bacon put together his own army.

Nathaniel Bacon waged war on the Pamunkey, who were an Algonquian speaking tribe friendly to colonists and part of the Powhatan **chiefdom.** Governor Berkeley told Bacon to stop. The Pamunkey people left their village and hid in a nearby swamp. Bacon continued to attack other

American Indians, even if they were friendly toward the English colonists. Governor Berkeley proclaimed that Nathaniel Bacon was an outlaw. Bacon attacked Jamestown and took over the capitol. He then followed the Pamunkey into the swamp and killed many of the remaining warriors. Bacon took the survivors to Jamestown and held them captive.

A few weeks later, Bacon suddenly became sick and died, and Governor Berkeley returned to Jamestown. In 1677, Berkeley wrote a new treaty for the Powhatan tribes. It still stated that the tribes were under English rule. The treaty also established new **reservations** for each tribe, and the tribes were now required to pay taxes to the governor of Virginia.

Here Bacon (right) is shown arguing with Governor Berkeley (left). Bacon's rebellion did more to harm relations between the colonists and Virginia's Indians, just as Governor Berkeley had feared.

FUR TRADE AND GREAT WARRIOR PATH

American Indians west of the Blue Ridge Mountains in Virginia traded furs with French trappers in the Ohio River Valley. American Indian tribes fought among themselves for control of the fur trade. In a treaty in 1744, in order to promote peace and the fur trade, the Virginia and Pennsylvania governors agreed to let the American Indians, including the Iroquois to the north, travel freely along the Great Warrior Path (map page 8). They had to promise not to attack settlers on the east side of the Blue Ridge Mountains.

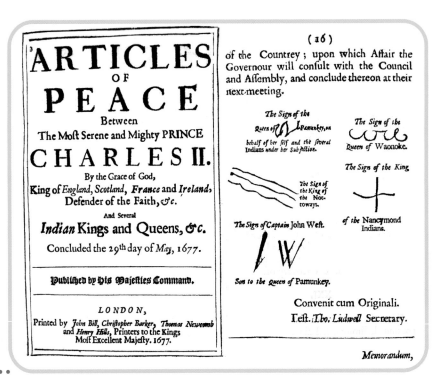

*The treaty signed between the Virginian colonists and Indians in 1677 is sometimes known as the Treaty of Middle **Plantation**. Some of the signatures of tribal leaders are visible here (right). One of the conditions of the treaty made the leaders subjects of the king of England.*

FRENCH AND INDIAN WAR, 1754–1763

In 1754, the French and British went to war in North America. Because the French treated them better and did not have the strong desire to colonize the region, Iroquois Indians helped the French and attacked English towns and settlements all along the Valley of Virginia. English settlers were killed and kidnapped by warriors from various tribes of the Ohio River Valley. Virginia's Governor Robert Dinwiddie sent George Washington and the Virginia **militia** to help British troops fight the French and Indians.

Great Britain eventually won the war and claimed the land west of the Blue Ridge Mountains. The king of England said that the new land would be given to the American Indians. However, the pioneer settlers ignored this and forced the American Indians to move farther west. As a result, the Great Warrior Path soon became the Great Wagon Road, with European settlers traveling north and south in western Virginia. In time, the remaining American Indians were forced out of the western part of Virginia.

This silver badge was made in the late 1600s. Indians visiting English settlements had to wear badges like this, which served as passports.

RESERVATIONS

Peace treaties made between the Virginia colony and American Indian tribes in the 1600s and 1700s created **reservations,** which was a European idea. But the reservations did not give American Indians enough land on which to survive. The best land near the rivers now belonged to the British. European settlers were also destroying forests by cutting down trees to build homes and fences, and the American Indian **culture** depended on those forests for food, clothing, and shelter.

Virginia's American Indians struggled to survive. Many tribes left Virginia to join larger groups elsewhere. Many of the American Indians who stayed tried to blend in with the new European cultures. They sometimes married white settlers and took English names, in order to survive in the changing world around them. Because of this, almost all American Indian cultures and **traditions** died out over time.

By the 1800s, there were only four remaining reservations in Virginia. By 1878, all but two of the reservations were gone. Few of Virginia's American Indians survived in what had been their homeland for hundreds of years. In 1940, the U.S. **census** showed only 198 American Indians living in Virginia. However, some of Virginia's native peoples remained and fought to continue their cultures. The last two reservations in Virginia, the Mattaponi and Pamunkey, still exist and are the oldest in the United States.

Virginia Tribes Today

Today there are eight recognized tribes in Virginia. They are the Nansemond, Rappahannock, Chickahominy, Eastern Chickahominy, Mattaponi, Upper Mattaponi, Pamunkey, and Monacan. All of these tribes can trace their history back nearly 400 years. All of the tribes except the Monacan were part of the Algonquian speaking Powhatan Nation. The Monacan were one of the Siouan tribes of Virginia.

NANSEMOND

In 1607, when Jamestown was settled, the Nansemond lived in what is now Suffolk, along the Nansemond River. The tribe's population was about 1,000 people, with 200 to 300 warriors. The Nansemond moved several times as colonial settlers forced them from their lands. They were living on the Nottoway River in 1792, when they sold their last 300 acres of **reservation** land.

Nansemond Assistant Chief Earl "War Chief" Bass (left) and Nansemond Chief Barry "Big Buck" Bass (right) are taking part in the Grand Entry during a recent powwow in Suffolk, Virginia.

The Nansemond Indian Tribal Association was recognized by the Virginia General Assembly in 1984. It is one of the remaining Algonquian tribes of the Powhatan. The Nansemond Indian Tribal Association works to keep the Nansemond **culture** alive through projects, events, and a yearly powwow.

RAPPAHANNOCK

The word *Rappahannock* means "where the tide ebbs and flows." The Algonquian Rappahannock were part of the Powhatan Nation. The Rappahannock moved their tribal villages many times, and English settlers took over their lands illegally many times. In the 1670s, the Virginia General Assembly set up a reservation for the Rappahannock at Indian Neck. As with other tribes, much of the land was sold when the reservation was split into individual ownership at the end of the 1800s.

Rappahannock Chief Anne Richardson is the first female chief since 1647. She is pictured here standing in front of the Rappahannock Cultural Center.

The present-day Rappahannock tribe owns about 140 acres of land in Indian Neck. The Rappahannock maintain a tribal government and headquarters there. Their Rappahannock Cultural Center displays historic **artifacts** and has an archive (preserved collection) of tribal records.

CHICKAHOMINY

Chickahominy means "Coarse Ground Corn People." The Chickahominy were the Powhatan tribe located closest to the Jamestown settlement in 1607. Their main villages were along the Chickahominy River, on the north side of the James River. The Chickahominy was one of the first tribes forced out of its villages by colonial settlers in the 1600s.

The Chickahominy later moved back to their homeland near Charles City County and reorganized as a tribe in 1900. Tribal members bought land and farms near their traditional homeland, and today they own about 25,000 acres. The Chickahominy Tribe is presently the largest in Virginia, with about 1,000 members. The Chickahominy built a tribal center in 1972. This building is used for business meetings and community gatherings. Chickahominy children meet at the tribal center on Saturdays to learn more about their **culture,** including pottery, beadwork, leather craft, dancing, and tribal history, all taught by members of the tribe. Each year, the Chickahominy host a fall festival and powwow.

EASTERN CHICKAHOMINY

The Eastern Chickahominy Tribe split from the larger Chicahominy Tribe in 1925. The Eastern Chickahominy Tribe has about 150 members, and is located about 25 miles east of Richmond. About 75 members live in a small community near Windsor Shades, in New Kent County. They have a tribal church and hold tribal council four times a year. Each year, the Eastern Chickahominy hold a festival celebrating their culture and **heritage.**

MATTAPONI

The Mattaponi was one of the six Algonquian speaking tribes that Chief Powhatan originally **inherited.** The Mattaponi **Reservation** dates back to colonial days. It is located near West Point, Virginia, where the Mattaponi and Pamunkey Rivers meet to form the York River. Today, the Mattaponi Tribe has about 100 members. The Mattaponi have a museum and education trading

The education trading post on the Mattaponi reservation includes a reconstructed longhouse. Visitors can see how longhouses were made.

post on their reservation. Members of the tribe have been active in helping Virginia school children understand their **traditions** and heritage, which they've hung onto for 400 years.

UPPER MATTAPONI

The Upper Mattaponi are **descendants** of Indians of the Mattaponi and Pamunkey reservations. These people settled in King William County on the Upper Mattaponi River. The Upper Mattaponi built the Sharon Indian School around 1919. In 1964, the school was closed when schools in Virginia were **integrated.**

In 1987, the Sharon Indian School and its surrounding two acres of land were returned to the tribe. The school is now used as a tribal meeting place. Today, the Upper Mattaponi Tribe has about 100 members. They hold an annual spring festival sharing their culture and history with their children and community.

Pamunkey

The Pamunkey had the most powerful warriors of all the Algonquian tribes under Chief Powhatan's control. The Pamunkey fought bravely to keep their lands in the early 1600s. In 1658, the Virginia General Assembly set aside **reservation** lands for the Pamunkey.

Today, more than 100 members live on the Pamunkey Reservation, located in King William County along the Pamunkey River. They are involved in preserving the **habitat** of the river life. They also work to preserve their past and operate a museum on the reservation. The Pamunkey is one of the few Virginia tribes that has practiced pottery making continuously for hundreds of years.

This painted pottery was made in the 20th century by students at the Pamunkey pottery school. The Pamunkey still carry on this tradition today.

Monacan

The Monacan people were Siouan speakers who lived in the Piedmont region for hundreds of years, before moving toward the Blue Ridge Mountains in the late 1600s. In 1833, a Monacan named William Johns purchased land at Bear Mountain.

Today's Monacans are still at Bear Mountain in Amherst County, with more than 700 tribal members. They have opened a Living History Museum and Indian Village at Natural Bridge, Virginia, in order to preserve their **culture** and teach people about their **traditions** and history.

Algonquian Place-Names

Many names of places in Virginia are Algonquian words or tribal names. Here is a short list of some of the names that are still used today:

Chesapeake = "great shellfish bay"

Potomac = "river of the great swans"

Rappahannock = "rise and fall of water"

Shenandoah = "beautiful daughter of the stars"

Nansemond = "fishing point or angle"

Poquoson = "swamp"

AMERICAN INDIAN INFLUENCE

It is impossible to understand Virginia today without studying its history and the stories of the many cultures that have lived here and influenced the state. The American Indians were the first people to live in Virginia. Only with their help could the first Europeans have established a successful colony at Jamestown.

Unfortunately, the Europeans who continued to come to America did not return those first favors of the Powhatan. Despite years of broken treaties, land theft, and poor treatment, however, some of the original American Indian cultures of Virginia have survived. We still benefit from their knowledge and traditions, and they continue to be an important part of Virginia's modern population. We are reminded of Virginia's first people in our everyday lives, through the food we eat and the names of places we live.

Monacan Chief Kenneth W. Branham stands holding a war club at the Indian Village at Natural Bridge, Virginia.

Map of Virginia

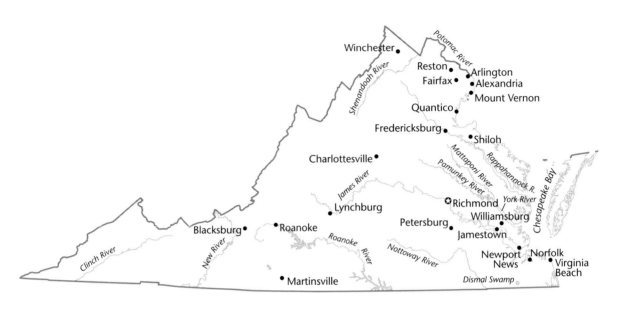

Winchester

Potomac River

Reston
Arlington
Fairfax
Alexandria
Mount Vernon

Quantico

Fredericksburg

Shiloh

Shenandoah River

Charlottesville

Mattaponi River

Rappahannock R.

Pamunkey River

Chesapeake Bay

James River

Lynchburg

Richmond

York River

Williamsburg

Blacksburg

Roanoke

Petersburg

Jamestown

New River

Roanoke River

Nottoway River

Newport News

Norfolk

Virginia Beach

Clinch River

Martinsville

Dismal Swamp

CANADA

ME
VT
NH
NY
MA
MI
CT
RI
PA
NJ
IN
OH
MD
DE
WV
KY
Virginia
TN
NC
SC
AL
GA
FL

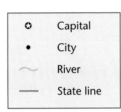

✪	Capital
•	City
～	River
—	State line

N
W   E
S

0   100 mi.

Timeline

ca. 13,000 B.C.E.	Earliest people first come to Virginia.
C.E. 1584	John White comes to America with English explorers and draws and describes the native peoples.
1607	Jamestown settlers arrive from England.
1608	John Smith is captured and taken to Chief Powhatan's village.
1609–1610	It is the winter of the "Starving Time" for Indians and colonists.
1614	Pocahontas marries John Rolfe, and peace between the English settlers and the Powhatan begins.
1617	Pocahontas sails with John Rolfe to England.
1618	Chief Powhatan dies. Opechancanough becomes chief.
1622	Opechancanough and warriors attack Jamestown settlers in what becomes known as the "Great Massacre."
1644	Opechancanough leads a second attack on Virginia colonists.
1646	Opechancanough is captured and killed by Jamestown colonists.
1676	Nathaniel Bacon attacks Piedmont Indians and leads a rebellion.
1677	Treaties take the last of the American Indian lands. **Reservations** are set up.
1744	Treaty gives American Indians the "right" to travel the Great Warrior Path.
1754–1763	The French and Indian War lasts until a peace treaty is signed in Paris in 1763. Many more Indians leave Virginia.
1763	King George III of England gives the land west of the Blue Ridge Mountains to the American Indians.
1940	U.S. **Census** shows only 198 American Indians left living in Virginia.
1964	**Integration** forces American Indian schools to close. Indian children attend public schools and colleges.
1983–1989	Eight American Indian tribes are finally recognized by the Virginia General Assembly.
2000	There are about 2,000 **descendants** of Virginia American Indians organized in tribal groups. Only about 200 of these live on the two oldest reservations in the United States, which are the Mattaponi and Pamunkey.

Glossary

afterlife life after death

ancestor someone who came earlier in a family

archaeologist someone who studies the lives of people in the past by examining the things they left behind. Archaeology is the study of the lives of people in the past.

artifact object made by humans, such as a tool, pottery, or weapon

buckskin strong, soft leather made from the skin of a deer

cane often hollow, thin, and somewhat flexible plant stem

census official count of the number of people in a place

ceremony special act or acts done on special occasions

chasm deep gap in the earth's surface

chiefdom group of tribes under one powerful ruler

clan group of families who have the same ancestor

confederation group of peoples joined for some purpose

cornhusk doll doll made from the husk, or outer covering, of corn

cradleboard small wooden frame to which an infant is strapped

culture way of life of a group of people, including their food, clothing, shelter, and language

descendant person who comes from a particular ancestor or family

elder person who has authority because of age and experience

environment surrounding conditions and forces that affect living things

epidemic outbreak and rapid spread of disease to many people

extinct no longer living

fall line last set of waterfalls in a river before it reaches sea level. Fresh water meets salt water below this point. In Virginia, the fall line separates the Coastal Plain and Piedmont regions.

fiber threadlike parts that form the tissue of plants and animals.

flint hard stone that can be shaped with repeated chipping

forage search for something, such as food

gamble play a game in which something, such as money, is risked for the chance of gain

gourd fruit from a vine related to the pumpkin and melon

habitat place where a plant or animal lives in nature

herb plant or part of plant used in medicine or in seasoning foods

heritage something handed down from the past or from one's ancestors

Ice Age period of time when a large part of the earth was covered with glaciers, which are huge sheets of moving ice

immunity power to resist infection

inherited received by right from a person at his or her death

integrated made open to all races

jasper usually red, green, brown, or yellow stone used to make ornamental objects

jerky long, sun-dried slices of preserved meat

lacrosse ball game played outdoors using a long-handled stick with a net for catching, throwing, and carrying the ball

marsh area of wet land usually overgrown with grasses and similar plants

mica mineral that easily breaks into very thin sheets

migrate move from one region to another, or pass from one region to another on a regular schedule

militia group of citizens with some military training called to fight in emergencies. Members of the militia were called militiamen.

mussel shellfish with a soft body inside two shells hinged together, often used as food

plantation large farm on which the farm workers live

reed tall, thin grass found in wet areas

reservation land set aside by the government to be used by American Indians

ritual established form for a ceremony or a system of rites

rush grasslike marsh plant with hollow stems

smallpox very contagious and serious disease that causes a fever and sores on the skin

smoke expose to smoke to give flavor and keep from spoiling; usually done with meat

soapstone soft stone having a soapy or greasy feeling

surveyor person who surveys, or records measurements of the earth's surface

sweat lodge hut heated by steam from water poured on hot stones and used by American Indians for healing

tradition belief or custom handed down from one generation to another

tuckahoe type of plant used as food by American Indians

turquoise greenish-blue stone used in jewelry

More Books to Read

Ansary, Mir Tamim. *Eastern Woodlands Indians.* Chicago, Ill.: Heinemann Library, 2000.

Boraas, Tracey. *The Powhatan: A Confederacy of Native American Tribes.* Mankato, Minn.: Capstone, 2002.

Rountree, Helen C. *Young Pocahontas in the Indian World.* Yorktown, Va.: J & R Graphics Services, 1995.

Shaughnessy, Diane. *Pocahontas, Powhatan Princess.* New York, N.Y.: Rosen, 1998.

Williams, Suzanne Morgan. *Powhatan Indians.* Chicago, Ill.: Heinemann Library, 2003.

Index

About the Author

Karla Smith grew up in a navy family and moved several times before settling down in Suffolk, Virginia. She has been teaching third, fourth, and fifth graders social studies since 1969. When she is not teaching, Smith enjoys exploring Virginia's waters in a sailboat.